SEPTEMBER, 1902.

THE STAGE — ADELINE STANHOPE WHEATCROFT

The Young Men's Home Journal

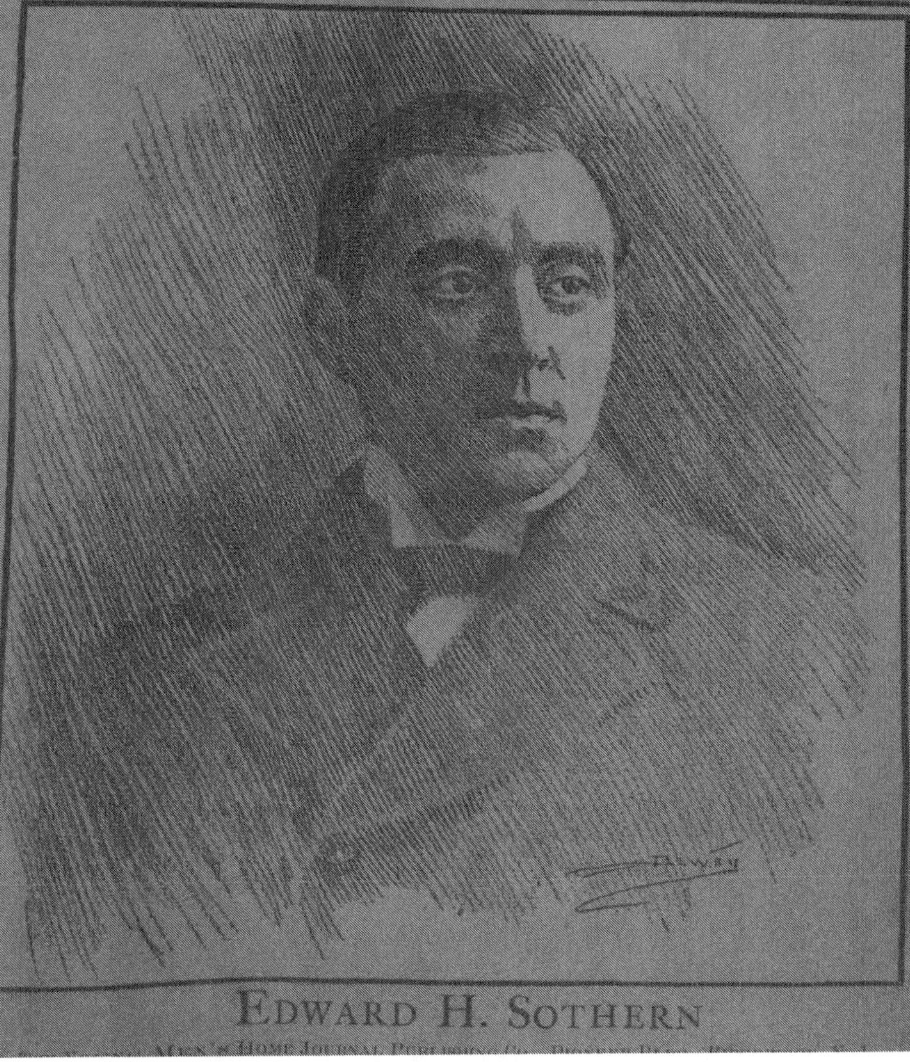

EDWARD H. SOTHERN

Men's Home Journal Publishing Co.

WILL YOU RENT YOUR BRAINS?

We pay MONEY for IDEAS and THINGS. We want

Jokes

Funny Stories

Amateur Photographs

Original Short Stories

Articles of Special Interest to Men

Suggestions for Improving This Magazine

People to Secure New Subscribers, et cetera.

WE pay handsomely for the above. Write and tell us what you have to offer. Read the magazine over carefully and you may be able to suggest something valuable alike to us and yourself. Some people can originate but cannot execute. Give us the ideas and if we use them we will pay you. We intend soon to open a department in this magazine entitled——

NEW WAYS TO MAKE MONEY

Can you suggest something along this line? Write to the Editor as often and as long as you please. Your letters will have prompt attention.

The Young Men's Home Journal

Editorial Office, 24 West 22nd Street, New York City.

Volume II SEPTEMBER 1902 Number 1

THE YOUNG MEN'S HOME JOURNAL

CONTENTS

Cover Design *by Alfred J. Dewey*

THE YOUNG MEN'S HOME JOURNAL IS A MONTHLY MAGAZINE FOR MEN, EDITED BY GRENVILLE KLEISER.

Subscription price. One Dollar a year.   Single copies. Ten Cents.

THE AMERICAN NEWS COMPANY, AGENTS.
39 Chambers Street, NEW YORK.

ADDRESS

The Young Men's Home Journal
Twenty-four West Twenty-second Street.
NEW YORK CITY.

PIONEER BUILDING, RIDGEWOOD, NEW JERSEY.

Adeline Stanhope Wheatcroft

THE STAGE AS A VOCATION

by ADELINE STANHOPE WHEATCROFT

WHEN a boy begins to leave off growing out of his clothes, and doesn't want to "play"—but instead, ,sionally seen to sit thinking, ᴜming, as he quietly kicks the pᴇ ᴇs, or the grass, or the fox terrier, it is apt to suddenly dawn on those immediately interested in that boy's welfare, that the time has come to choose his field in the battle of life. Shall he be soldier, sailor, or civilian? Shall he be made into a lawyer, doctor, clergyman, or embryo merchant; shall those dear, beautiful eyes be ruined, in spite of protecting green shades, by following columns of figures by night and day; shall he be painter, sculptor, poet, or musician? In short, which star in the firmament of hope shall he make his goal? He must do something to earn his living. He has never known anything but comfort, nay luxury, but the time is at hand when he must assert his own individuality — his independence, manhood; be something and someone. Each career is suggested in turn, the ground well thrashed out, the pros and cons well weighed and advised on, and at the end of it all, the boy says: "I am going to be an actor, and I am going to be a good one!" Of course he fully realizes that the fuss recently made by the Pelee Mountain is as nothing to the havoc his declaration will make among his friends and family to the third and fourth generation of his fourteenth and fifteenth cousins! But his mind is made up and he comes of stock that doesn't go back on its convictions! The wish is father to the thought and in spite of opposition and prejudice he will put the thought into execution.

There are boys who are content to plod; to work their way up slowly & laboriously in the routine of an office; but there are others who can never become reconciled to such a life, and our boy is one of these. He craves freedom of thought, space for his new, young ambitions and original ideas. Having been well brought up, he has knowledge of right and wrong, plenty of will-power to keep within bounds, and too much pride to abuse the glorious privilege of freedom.

Now let us see his chances of success.

The prejudice against the stage is fast dying out! Its followers, instead of being looked upon as "Rogues & Vagabonds" as in the days of Good Queen Bess, are envied, courted, entertained, even knighted! And the ranks of the Dramatic Profession are constantly being swelled by recruits from "social" circles, who find in their new environment scope for their unusual talent, adaptability, ambition and breadth of vision.

In favor of the stage, it must be urged that larger salaries may be earned in a shorter space of time than in almost any other profession or business; that while its lower ranks are more or less crowded with mediocrity, there is a large, clear space at the top for those with capability & patience to reach it. There is a fascination, too, in giving pleasure and instruction to others; of always looking and moving forward. When once an actor has commanded recognition, it rests with himself alone to hold his position.

The best theatrical managers of to-day want youth, ambition, culture, & gentlemanly bearing in the actors they employ; they need new blood, coupled with more *savoir faire* than obtained in the ranks of what are still fondly alluded to by a handful of old actors and their adherents as the "palmy days of the Drama." Oh! those poor dear old palms, could they be transplanted how they would wither & die in the rarified atmosphere of our modern advancement!

When I have advocated a career on the stage for young men, the response has come not infrequently, "Oh, naturally! you have a dramatic school." Yes! — but I have a dramatic school because I advocate a dramatic career! It is self-evident that under the new regime a man must have adequate training before he can apply to a manager for a position. Some of my pupils after holding good positions as actors, have entered the managerial ranks,

achieved success, and apply to me regularly for my graduates.

The old way of carrying on a spear and waiting to "work yourself up" is mercifully entirely superannuated. Time was, when a young man had to begin at the bottom of the ladder and be content to spend months and years carrying a hammer, or speaking a few syllables, in short "Supering" as it was called, putting up with the temper and profane language of uneducated supermasters and stage managers, dressing in crowded rooms, with specimens of humanity as uncouth as they were unclean. In this way, and standing with this unpalatable crowd in the wings of the theatre, able only to see the back & helmet of the man immediately in front of him, he was fondly supposed to learn the great art of acting! No wonder, poor boy, he was glad enough to get away from the stifling odors that environed him, and take refuge in the "public house" or "saloon" and there vent his grievances and dreams of what might have been, or ought to be, to sympathetic, if beery listeners! It sounds well to say "I rose from the ranks" — but by the time you have achieved anything like a reputation, you have lost the best years of your life, become embittered, selfish, and jealous of the success of others, & have lost the sweetest blessings of life — Faith and Hope.

Now note the difference.

A course of six months in a genuine dramatic school (there are schools and schools) is absolutely sufficient to enable you to secure and hold a good position, under first-class management. In surroundings artistic, congenial and refined you are enabled to improve your natural qualifications, acquaint yourself with stage technique, improve your walk, bearing, manner, speech and voice. You gain polish, and above all, are absolutely cured of self-consciousness a n d timidity.

Now, is not this worth while?

That the number of men se:king a stage career is smaller than that of women is due, in my opinion, to an insufficient & mistaken knowledge of the subject. This subject is second nature to me. Brought up with no knowledge of theatrical life, suddenly compelled to earn my living, I have from the age of sixteen found a stanch friend in the stage. I watched the progress of the time. I saw what was needed for the young aspirant to histrionic fame, based the fundamental principles of my school on those convictions, and carry it steadily on, assured that I can and do help every one who comes to me on the road to success. If you have any doubts as to the necessity of dramatic training just watch two young men at a first rehearsal, only one having taken instruction. I can say without vanity that my pupils are never a w k w a r d, or amateurish, are always self reliant and resourceful, and have the *cachet* of the "pro-. fessional." The dramatic school has another strong point: it proves unmistakably to those who have an unreasoning passion for acting, whether or not they have the necessary qualifications to back them up, and while in a six months

course they cannot fail to find their "own degree" as Shakespeare has it, they cannot help becoming in every way improved by its influence.

A would-be actor must be free from any serious defect of speech, voice, or physique, and should possess an ordinary general education. Incidentally, a knowledge of the French language is, as Richard Mansfield says, of considerable service on the stage. He should moreover possess a keen imagination, & a desire to portray the thoughts and personality of beings of fancy.

Now we come to the oft reiterated trials, hardships, temptations, etc. All nonsense! A man and woman wishing to pursue the straight and narrow path can do so fully as well on the stage as off it. In the same way, if their views of life run in an opposite direction, the fact that they are not on the stage will not keep them pure. As for the hardships, I for one could never find them. There is work, true! But "work is the salt that savors life." To be anything, you must work, and a stage life saves you from ennui and boredom, while it brings you appreciation, r e c o g n i t i o n, scope for your ambition, self respect, & independence. A man can lead as upright a life on the stage as off, and more so, for indulgence and dissipation will affect his work so soon that he will be brought up suddenly by nature with a good round turn and be made to realize that art is a jealous mistress and will tolerate no rival.

Upon entering either a dramatic school or the theatrical profession, exercise self-restraint. Keep your own counsel. Observe. Beware of petty jealousies. Don't form sudden and intimate friendships. Don't criticise your instructors or stage managers until you are as familiar with the subject as they are. Refuse absolutely to be discouraged because you meet with temporary disappointment. Make it a rule to save half your salary every week. Set your objective point high up, and work steadily up to it, never looking back, & when you become an actor and rehearsals are over for a time, and your work hours are in the evening, don't loaf all day, don't perpetually frequent the "Rialto," but read, exercise, study a little, and when your evening's work is over, after a reasonable time, go to bed. Don't sit up till the small hours and feel wretched and unfit for anything in the morning. Remember you owe a great deal to your friends, your emyloyers, your art, and to yourself.

Upon entering on your coveted career, probably your first obstacle will be your youth. They will say you are "immature," "inexperienced" etc. Never mind, the very people who tell you so would give all they possess to recall their own lost youth.

Again, if old actors try to discourage you, and perhaps ridicule your ambitions and efforts, & throw a slur on dramatic schools in general, and yours in particular, bear with them, be merciful, remember they are old, you young. They had not your advantages years ago. They have worked hard & may be footsore and weary. You can afford to be forbearing, for are you not sure-

ly mounting, while they are feebly clinging to the downward rungs of the ladder?

That the stage has its abuses is not to be denied and is to be deplored. But where is the calling that can boast of such purity that it can with impunity "throw the stone?" Were the x-rays of public criticism directed as intently in other directions, who shall say but that poor abused Thespis would not emerge the whitest of them all!

It takes more than one swallow to make a summer, & while you may have read of a few glaring blots on the 'scutcheon, I could fill a volume telling you of the acts of gentleness, help, charity, forgiveness & mercy done by people of the stage, not only to those of their own calling, but to men and women not labelled "actor" and "actress," but whose acts would break up homes, hearts and lives "did they but know."

A dramatic school cannot perfect you as an actor, but it *can* rub off the rough edges, give you a vast amount of necessary information, eradicate your faults, point out your strong and weak points, and fit you to claim the right to a foothold on the ladder to fame. You will have been through the fire, and will have patience, perseverance, faith, hope, determination, & your own brave heart to hold you in readiness to embrace Opportunity when she knocks at your door.

If the stage is so hard a life, why do actors give their sons a fine education and then put them on the stage? See for example Robert Edeson, Arthur Byron, Joseph Wheelock, Thomas Whiffin, Ethel and

Lionel Barrymore, Joseph and William Jefferson, Maud Adams, Viola Allen, John Drew, whose daughter has just entered the profession after a course of study with me, and scores of others. Look at Edward H. Sothern, son of the great Lord Dundreary Sothern: who shall say he is not actor, scholar and gentleman? An enthusiast in his work, he is always ready and anxious to give a helping hand to beginners, always on the alert for a glimpse of genius. He not only is a patron of my school, but gives practical proof of his faith in it by constantly engaging my graduates. Only a few weeks ago his manager, Mr. Daniel Frohman, signed a contract with Gordon Johnstone, one of the clever men in the school last winter.

The stage opens a bright gateway to success in life & at this moment I am unable to supply the demands of managers for young men with training and the other necessary qualifications.

If I may be permitted a word to parents, it will be this: Should your child show intense love for the stage, a longing to act, you may as well give in soon as late. It is a fire that will not be quenched. Thwart him, force him to devote himself to other work, his spirit will rebel, or faint, and in either case his future will be ruined, & in all probability in after years, after failing at everything else, he will go on the stage in spite of you, and to his own ruin, having worn away hope, ambition, enthusiasm & youth in an endeavor to please you and do his duty, as you have shown it to him.

Doctors and lawyers have given up the profession uncongenial to them, and come to me (sometimes with their wives) for stage training and have succeeded. Even clergymen not infrequently come for the benefit to their own work that the study affords.

That a young actor may meet with setbacks & disappointments goes without saying. Which of us has not his cross to bear sooner or later? Unkind criticism, anxiety & disappointment come alike to the doctor, the lawyer and the priest. Fame and suffering often go hand in hand, but the greater the difficulty, the grander the victory.

Ask Mr. Sothern if he would change his life for one of idleness. And the next time he plays *Hamlet*, if you have a soul for poetry, thought or art, don't fail to see and note his work.

Concentrate on the Now.
THE PAST IS GONE AND YOU
CAN DO MORE IN THE FUTURE
WHEN IT BECOMES THE NOW

Talks With Men.

by *MARION HUNT.* *

I HAVE always been fond of proverbs, and knowing this, my friends sometimes take the trouble to copy a few. I should like to give this which follows to all the American young men. It will tell them exactly of their need.

Taking a bird's-eye view of the men in this country I should say that there is one essential, national vice. There is no faith. In fact, we Americans have no belief in the magnificence of faith. We are brought up on a money-basis. We have been told to suspect the world. The sweetest & most delicate and wholesome natures are marred by this blemish of suspicion. Where shall we get our Gallileos, our Tolstois and our Teslas, if we cramp imagination by trustlessness? I mention Tesla, especially, because he has the most splendid trust that was ever incarnated in a human. He is a Man. More than this, he is a Great Man. But you don't know him.

Now, the quotation I refer to, is this; & it was taken from the wise thoughts of Kong, who is known as Confucius: "A youth when at home, should be filial; and abroad, respectful to elders. He should be earnest and trustful. He should overflow in love to all, & cultivate

the friendship of the good."

I quote the above for the one word. He should be trustful.

++   ++

"But how can a man be trustful when he is surrounded by enemies?" This question was asked of an elderly Southern priest, who knew the world. He replied: "Believe that all men are your friends, but act as tho' all men are your enemies."

But there is, I think, a closer and better explanation in that voice which is heard through 2300 years. (Can men really lose their great teachers? Not one has been forgot. They must have been beloved men.) Confucius says: "At fifteen I had my mind bent upon learning. At 30 I stood firm. At 40 I had no doubts. At 50 I knew the decrees of Heaven. At 60 my ear was an obedient organ for the reception of truth," and "See what a man does. Mark his motives: examine in what thing he rests."

You see that knowledge bases faith. "Get knowledge; and with your knowledge get understanding."

++   ++

I have often thought that a good man must have had either a good father or a good mother. But I see there is another class. He may be born a great soul. Like water-lilies, virtue may spring out of the mud.

---

*Miss Hunt's address is— PHILLIPSBURG P. O., New Jersey, R. F. D. 2.

There is another thing I would say to Americans— the most wonderful of all people. I note that business men are not always perfectly trained in intrinsic courtesy. There is such a thing as business courtesy, scientific courtesy and plain fine manners. This last is common and the rule: the second is scarce to find, and the first is not often to be found. The first is deficiency, the one most noticed by Europeans. They put us down as an ill bred nation. That is not the case. We are a superior people. We can beat them to pieces with our fine mechanisms. But we were brought up to shake the world. Our spirit is aggressive in its politeness. We are acquainted with thieves and tyrants and have saved business by our wit. The truth is, that there is not a marked and systematic Lincoln business honesty at the basis of business dealings. So, you see, it seems impossible to practise all virtues in the business courtesy. Business transaction has become a very sharp game — appearing to lack delicacy. On general lines we are the most delicate people in the world! the most charming, the cleverest, most sensitive and healthy of the nations. We can do in one day what England will do in six.

But I tell you, men, you can stand a great deal of cultivation yet.

Speaking of cultivation: There is such a thing as overtraining.

I had the privilege of looking over a pretty letter written by a young woman just out of France. She was very polite, and very naturally was very polite, and very naturally kind. She was making a few gifts to the family and kept saying, "if you will kindly accept it." I was almost amused — and yet, it was a pretty letter. "If you will kindly accept it!" What in the name of sense did she offer anything not sure to please? But then — it was just a little example of what over-training will do. Education is a fine thing. Do not doubt it. I speak for education. It will solve much to a young man. But before you get education, get common-sense: and take care not to lose it, for it is easy to lose and very hard to find. The true man is a mine of common-sense.

When you receive a letter see that you do one thing. Seize the spirit and let the letter take care of itself. You may be receiving from a philosopher who means no harm, but has not all sail to the wind. If such is the case, you may be wounded for nothing: and you cannot afford to waste your energy.

Time is money.

Here is another very pretty little Chinese proverb. "The cautious seldom err." I would supplement that by saying, the suspicions may err: great, habitual cautiousness leads to actual suspiciousness. Again, I say, get more knowledge and try to trust. In my opinion, trust is the most beautiful of the godly qualities. The reason I like it so much is because I do not see any of it, anywhere. My world is a big desert. A faithless society is damnable! That is strong language. But I could pile a few more curses on the utter damnableness of Social Distrust! An Ass! An Ass! Have I not told you not to string flowers on the necks of plain donkeys?

"With coarse rice to eat, with water to drink, and my bended arm for a pillow, I have still joy in the midst of these things."

So said Confucius. And so say I. Love! Love! in the midst of Death. I shall devote my strength, my mind, my soul to Thee, thou sweet, simple Mother of Wants! "Come back to Nature" is going to be the watch-word of the whole world, presently. I would be a John the Baptist, if I could be. But be assured,— there will be a Jesus. There are commanding figures yet to be born. My only grief is, that I shall not live to the year 2000. No! I must die— so they tell me. But I believe nothing of it because I don't realize it. We never believe anything we can't realize. The facts, tho' are against.

"I would rather have a good friend than all the delights and treasures of Darius," said Plato. So say I, provided it may be got easy-fashion. But the risks are too large if it requires long journeys. I will tell you something. There was once a man. He was a moderately good man. He was surely a great man. Some thought he looked like a genius. He wanted a "good friend." So he said, "It cannot be a woman, because I shall have to marry her in order to keep her secure: and maybe, after I have secured her she might find a way out. So I will take a man for my friend."

10

This genius went into the prison, where a young fellow was confined for a slight cause. The elder said to the younger, "I want you to love me. Do you think you can do it?"

And the younger man fell on his neck and swore he was his brother. The elder got papers to prove that this brother was a new man. He freed him. He gave him a place in his house. He was good, gentle and beneficent. One day the younger was sent off on a special errand. "Go," said the elder, "and carry a message to a woman who delights me." The younger went, but he carried off the woman. Ergo!— go to the moon for your true friends: that is, unless you can find a man or woman made out of pieces of the angels. If they are a Heavenly Mosaic — that's different. Those may be mothers, but uncriticising, absolutely unspoiled friends are much rarer than unspoiled lovers.

And this reminds me. I will tell you about a spoiled lover and how she came white again. It is in verse and was suggested to me by a little, incident recorded by the newspapers — those great Spiritual Recorders! The poem is called——

Her Voice: or

LOVE'S RECOGNITION

Her voice! I heard it in the sea.
It was her lovely voice to me.
Her voice!— that tremor of the air.
Pure Heaven — it had anchored
    there.
Her voice! I heard its breathing soul
Within the lily's noiseless bowl.
I could not be deceived— I heard
The invincible and darling word.

I knew the burden of thy prayer.
　O Love, I heard thee — every-
　　where!

Her voice! The hills have bound it
　fast.
A slough about my spirit's cast.
Her voice! O bird — it did me wrong.
I cannot hear me in her song.
Her voice! the note that sang for me
Is lost upon the waiting sea.
Gone — flowing out from me, in fear
　That on its joy I pour a tear.
Thou dear, dead love — I could not
　shed
　Dishonor on thy shining head!

I heard a cry upon the sea, —
　Her voice! as tho' it spoke with
　　me.
A dreadful sob upon the air —
　I found her voice had broken there.
A sigh within the dying green,
　The subtle cry of things unseen —
Her voice. I thought I heard a moan
　In that poor grave, white daisy-
　　grown.
Her grief has crept within my
　breast —
　A bitter, an unheard unrest.

A bell came ringing through the air.
　I recognized that she was there.
I had been sleeping; oh, the thrall
　Of her missed, vocal madrigal.
I heard — it close and closer drew
　And breathed upon my breath
　　anew.
The perfume touched my stagnant soul
　Conversant with a lover's dole.
I tried in vain to understand
　My lover's hand upon my hand.

The earth was full of her I sought.
　Alas! she was and she was not.

I roused, and saw her glory shine —
　A glory that I knew was mine —
Upon the flowers. It crept upon
　The grave. I looked — the place
　　was gone.
But yet, I saw her not, and woe
　Mixed as a shadow in my glow.
Then out of lethargy I woke
　And to my invisible Lover spoke.
" Where art Thou? Speak, thou
　godly dream
　Or is it that thou dost but seem?
I fear. My joys have died so long
　I cannot quite believe the song."
And rested. Eagerly I heard
　The throb of her ineffable word.
" I lived — and died: and died to live.
　Too stained — to Thee I dared
　　not give
The broken stem, the wound, the sigh,
　The bitter blight of agony.
But purged by death I pray thee
　fold
　Me once within thy arms of gold."
I listened. She grew faint, — I
　pressed
　Her stricken head upon my breast.
I felt the terror of old pain
　Had coursed upon her soul, again.
I kissed it off. Content she stayed —
　As simple as a little maid.
Nor did she leave me; and her smile
　Has broken up the weary mile.
Her voice! ah, God — come back to
　me —
　Across the Burden of the Sea.

You see there is a great revenge
saved up by Nature for the unceles-
tial lover. God knows love is a
pretty thing. So he put it at the
top of all the other virtues to keep
clean and rare. I was saying to a
young man some time ago that

there is a great theory of "spiritual mates," abroad: and up to a certain point I believed in it. I said, "Why is it you are not getting ready for the Her? He looked abashed. He was a wicked & unregulated man. "Yes." I said, "I think intuitive folks are very thoughtful on that point. But the memory, if there is one, seems at last to fade, from sheer weariness and worldly misery. Why do you not live for the Her? I repeated, because I saw he was abashed. "What!" he gasped. "Yes," said I. "Well," he said, the Lord knows I don't know a woman from a woman. "Well, you're wicked," said I. "You're a Pagan." "Naught!" said he. "Is there a chance left?" "Well, yes!" I said, kind o' pitifully. "Of course. There's always chance in evolution. The Lord is that kind.

I hear he is married. It has been about six years. The woman in the case displays her husband as an example. Well, really! There's something one can do for another woman, altho' those dear women are such cats! —all but the maternal women and the large artistic folk, and the College girls, bless them! & some of the rare-headed business-women. Well, in fact, perhaps not more than half the women are cats. Bah! what scratchin'! I like velvet that *is* velvet! Give me the grand and comely gentleman (new school) about 120 miles to the wind-ward (Ship at anchor) as Robin Crusoe would say. The other combination's unnatural. I really think it has made me almost sleepy, talking so much about "lof," "lof," which one great man calls "devil," "devil."

Liar!— unwittingly, of course. Let us give every man glory until he has lost his last white feather.

∞ ∞

I will tell you a little story. It is quoted, but I hope it may be sufficiently new to most of you. It is very clever as well as very humorous.

Years ago there was a Queen and there was a doctor. The latter had a dog he doted upon. The Queen also admired the animal and asked for it, saying that if he would give it to her he should have whatever he asked for. . . . He gave it, and said, "Now, Madame, you promised to give me my desire." . . "I will," quoth she. . "Then, I pray you give me my dog again." Which she had to do for she had promised.

++ ++

Here is another pretty little smart retort which I must credit to Caesar. I say these smart things because I know what kind of men I am talking with. They love smartness. I am afraid they are even too smart, alas! The Americans are still young!

Here is the retort. Caesar was once pestered & scorned by a nobleman of a falling house. "You have no family!" said this ugly prig. "Ah," said Caesar, "My family begins where your family ends."

I tell you, men, old Caesar still lives! A great man *can't* die. And a great man, mind you, has capital Stuff in him.

* * *

Here is another little story which will show you how one great man turned an evil into a good. I will not quote literally.

When William the Conqueror landed on the soil of England, he inadvertently fell on the ground, which was an ill omen. Quick as thought he grasped a handful of the earth & held it aloft. "Thus do I seize England!" said he, proudly. And the troops hustled & established themselves.

Old Kong was right when he said: "The people may be made to follow a path of action, but they may not be made to understand it"

I do not know many men who can turn an evil into a good, but I know a few women. Women, you know, are naturally much cleverer. As I said, there is the cat element! Don't forget it. The cat is a smart animal. A woman is a subtle mind. She can beat a man with her little finger and he will say nothing; or if he says something, it will be like lyric poetry. It is very interesting, altho' I have only noticed the signs of the times. Men are great coquettes — nay, coxcombs — or else slovens: a few, decent and medium. And there are some pirates & savages. You're one of the half-dozen varieties. Take stock at once of your manners. That is one of the twenty-five occupations of civilization. But do not spend too much time that way.

* † *

And now I will give one little parting advice to the ambitious man. He wants fame. But what is that? Do you want notoriety? – scandal? Do you want something constantly to be expected of you? Do you want to be registered year by year? Do you want everybody, — yes, everybody to mind your business? Then get fame. But if you can be content with *success* you are a wise man.

Let fame to the dogs!

Here is something about a famous man. It is a little late in the day to make poetry in favor of our sad-eyed Neptune, but since no harm is intended to the dead & it is a good illustration of the theme, I beg you to read what I have written. You will see that success is the great idea: that fame is worldly damnation. I have called it ——

Love to Schley

Hero! You've suffered — who should know
 know
Better than we who share thy woe?
A curse upon thy poor brown hands,
Laid by ignominious commands.
But through that Storm this gold shall be
 be
That Public men have gloried thee.

Hero! You've suffered—common-sense
Shall be thy chiefest recompense.
Who led ships on that wrapping sea
And killed the mad catastrophe?
'Twas thee. Proud eagles at thy prow.
It was no less a soul than Thou.

Hero! You've suffered — but we hate
The Hate that will not compensate.
Men will not let your dear, white age
Be murdered by that recreant page.
Men will not blot the splendid glow
Of their large masterpieces so.
Hero! You're safe — upon the breast
That brought thee from eternal rest.
And to that rest, I say that thou
Shall journey with a cloudless brow!

Fame might be compared to a good piece of bacon crammed with maggots. I really do not think the meat is worth having. What is your opinion?

MAGAZINE CIRCULATION
As An Opening For Young Men With Ideas

Thoughts on The Subject by a Circulation Manager

MAGAZINE conditions have changed very greatly within the past ten years. Time was when an advertising manager with glib persuasiveness & bluster enough was the money maker for a publication. He is still; but talk & bluster serve him no longer unless backed by a solid circulation. Advertisers are themselves becoming experts, so that a publication with a circulation of less than 100,000—unless appealing to a special class—finds it a difficult matter to carry advertising enough to pay its way. A magazine without advertising patronage is on its way to death. Without circulation, its advertising manager is "The voice of one crying in the wilderness." The new conditions have made the circulation manager as important as the advertising manager, though the latter is still, & probably always will be, the strident fly that claims the credit for the dust the chariot causes.

In the magazine world there is now an unmet demand for men of energy and ideas to successfully devote their thought and time to the finding and holding of readers.

It costs money and a great deal of it to secure circulation rapidly. Even when money is spent circulation does not necessarily follow. I have in mind the case of one of the more recent of the cheap magazines which started out to win its way with a reputed cash appropriation of $50,000., all of which was spent in the course of a few weeks along only one line of publicity. The circulation did not arrive, thereupon the man who had spent this money put his wits to work and wrested victory from defeat by making every payment that came in help to pay proportionately for further publicity. The magazine has now a good standing. If the brains that he brought to bear, after lavish expenditure, had been called upon when he first started to throw the money out of the window, he would have saved himself nearly two years of worry and threatening failure.

It is so easy to spend money in noisy displays and startling announcements that the young man with money at hand is apt to think that success lies in that direction. About a year ago a circular was sent advertisers stating that a certain publication would during last winter mail three million letters sealed, or in other words, spend $60,000 in stamps. The argument made from this was that the circulation would at once jump into a leading position among the magazines of general literature. What happened? Well, in the first place the selection of names was left to a mailing agency which gathered the names from directories; or in other words, from the urban populations already surfeited with literary propositions. This was a fatal error, as the publication was designed for mail-order purposes. In the next place the three million letters were never mailed though tacitly the magazine had given the promise to advertisers that they would be mailed. In the third place, even those that were mailed did not produce commensurate results for the country buyer was omitted from the list. The counted chicken did not hatch; or at any rate its hatching was delayed. The egg may yet go addled. The young Napoleon of circulation who thought $60,000 in stamps would pave the way to success is still scurrying around looking for the needed circulation. Fortunately the business organization behind him is one of the largest in the country.

There are those who are inclined to try for circulation along the line made familiar to the public by the less reputable Baking Powder and the Tea and Coffee Companies who unload their products by giving away as a premium that which in itself appears to have as much value as the merchandise with which it is given away. I do not intimate that premiums are lacking in value; in fact one enormously successful publication in this country has been built up and is maintained on the premium basis. From the surface of things it would appear that others should be able to succeed in the same direction. The secret of this publication's success, however, is that it appeals to boys and the premiums that it gives away appeal also to boys, so that as a consequence there is a constantly recruited army of eager little workers maintained from year to year.

The general public, however, if it begins to be fed on premiums must be maintained on premiums, so that a publication once starting definitely on a premium line has commited itself to a road from which it is almost impossible to turn without meeting disaster. But even premiums will not always win a way, no matter how valuable. A publishing house of semi-religious fame, made its success in using books as premiums in its approaches to ministers, Sunday School workers and temperance people. Its offers fell absolutely flat, however, when made to professional men like doctors & lawyers. The latter particularly could not understand how a $5.00 book & a $3.00 magazine could both be honestly offered for $3.00. Not 2% would respond.

Within the past three years a variation of the premium business has been discovered and exploited. This variation consists in offering two, three or more publications, clubbed together, at a ridiculously low rate. The first year was a great success so far as producing individual takers was concerned, in fact one publication whose field of readers is necessarily limited reaped 75,000 subscriptions without stretching out a hand of effort itself, simply by quoting a very low rate to the publication that used it as a clubbing inducement. But what about the past season? There were more club-ing combinations in the field. The whimsical public objected to new subscriptions only being accepted at the clubbing rate, and the com-binations as a whole this past season have been failures, at which result circulation men who believe in every tub standing on its own bottom, ought to heartily rejoice. It will probably sound conservative and almost retrogressive for me to say that gift schemes, premium schemes, fourteen-months-for-twelve schemes, calender schemes etc., as a rule are poor methods of building up a circulation, for the in-evitable impression of the thinking public must be that in some form or another they pay for the extras that are thrown in and their only evident line of argument is to con-clude that the magazine itself is not worth the price asked for it.

I must not fail to speak warningly of The American News Company as a medium for circulation getting. It is not in the circulation business. It is a magnificently organized dis-tributer and collector. That is all. It is no Octopus, crushing out the life of those who trust it. It is sim-ply a machine whose workings are not understood by new circulation men. It takes 425,000 copies of one Philadelphia magazine and never returns a copy; it acts for every magazine of repute satisfactorily, with one or two exceptions where there is a shrewd suspicion of inten-tion to start a rival News Company. The News Company principle is a sound one, but the new magazine with small capital that thinks things are going swimmingly be-

cause the News Company takes 50,000 copies of the first issue is likely to have a rude awakening. Three or four months will elapse before a cent comes back, three edi-tions will have to be printed on Faith and Hope or Charity; every unsold copy will cost more to get back than it did to get out. Let the News Company demand arise, however, from a public demand that the magazine itself creates in-dependently, and this great organ-ization will be found to be the greatest possible aid in avoiding numberless accounts and escaping all bad ones. To show, however, the relative unimportance of the News Company, let me remind you that it reaches less than 10,000 Post Offices in the United States and Canada, while there are 85,000 Post Offices in all.

Set it down as a fact that there is no easy road or short cut to a per-manent circulation. Three im-portant elements enter into the getting of circulation. The first is to have a magazine worth the price; the second is to have it well adver-tised either by direct appeals or through the columns of other pub-lications; the third, and most diffi-cult essential, is to have the mag-azine recommended to others by word of mouth of subscribers or canvassers. A fourth might be ad-ded,—to create a feeling of friend-liness towards the magazine on the part of the subscriber, this to be secured by the utmost courtesy in all communications with the sub-scriber; particularly prompt & im-mediate courtesy whenever a com-plaint is received.

This brings me to that which in my opinion is an essential point in the career of a circulation man. I do not believe any circulation man should be trusted with the fate of a periodical unless he has worked up through the detail of inner organization of a subscription department so that he can keep his watch over the methods of handling the subscription after it is won. A circulation man is essentially a money spender; unless he produces results he has no reason for existence. If when he has gained a subscription a larger proportion than necessary of the money is spent in taking care of that subscription for 12 months, his own ability to continue spending money will be curtailed. Just to illustrate how vast a difference there is in methods, I might mention that one publication with about half a million subscribers spends very nearly 10 cents on each subscription in handling the same for one year, and another publication, of almost equally large subscription circulation, spends less than 5 cents on each subscription in handling it for one year. The difference between the two is $25,000, which money the circulation manager of the more economical magazine can feel free to use for further pushing, or which amount, if regarded as a dividend on an investment would represent four per cent on a capitalization of $625,000. These last figures will show the importance of economy in the office management, which economy is due solely to the fact that the circulation manager in question has been through long training in methods of internal organization. To illustrate the essential need of internal knowledge on the part of the circulation man, I will mention that one magazine, spending lavishly for circulars and circulation, has a head for the Premium Department, another for Club-raisers, another for newstand sales and another for subscription registration. The jealousies are persistent & very human; the results are constant jolts and many changes. One capable head, responsible for the circulation as a whole could make the magazine leap forward, for it is worth its price.

When a circulation manager has the necessary equipment for his task, and is a man of many ideas restrained by conservative & harsh self-judgment, and when he has found the magazine with which he wants to work, and incidently which wants him to work, he is unwise to attach himself to that magazine purely on a salary basis; he should make his arrangements on a commission basis with a drawing account. This makes his employer realize that his employee is only getting paid for results, and it stimulates the circulation man because of the inevitable profit for himself of constant and conscientious effort.

I shall not in this article speak of how a man can get along pleasantly with employers for whom he is spending large sums of money, for that sort of thing can never be imparted. He must simply learn not to be too sensitive about having his projects turned down, or his circulars torn to pieces; for it is not his own money he is spending. If he is convinced that the project is a good one he must learn to come up smiling after the rebuff and present the project from another point of view. Many a victory is won in circulation, as in life, on the second breath.

THE RELIGIOUS LIFE

conducted by
NOEL H. JACKS
General Secretary, Y. M. C. A. Hartford, Conn.

Questions concerning the religious problems of young men will be answered in this department.   Address all communications to Mr. Jacks, Drawer 10, Hartford, Conn.

MULTITUDES of young men to-day look askance at a religious life for them. They have altogether a wrong impression of what it means to be religious. In the popular mind a religious young man is one without much force of character; pale and feminine in personal appearance, & without physical ability; in a word "a sis-sy." They think to become religious means surrendering one's liberty to do as he pleases; to give up all pleasures, and business ambitions, and to live a life of self-denial and seclusion.

This wrong impression exists among young men to-day, as a re sult of men's efforts in the past and the present to associate a religious life with such outward charact-eristics as these. They were wrong then and are wrong now. Such a conception of a religious life never was formed in the Bible, but em-anated in the heart & brain of man. The young man of the Twentieth Century need not hesitate to reject it as spurious & false. This is what Jesus did. In his day, two thousand years ago, men prided themselves on being religious who were mak-ing the whole matter a thing of outward appearance and show. Jesus the founder of the higest type of religion the world has ever known said to these in His day: "Woe unto you, scribes, Pharisees, hypocrites! for ye are like unto whited sepulchres, which indeed ap-pear beautiful outward, but are within full of dead men's bones, and of all uncleanness even so ye al-so outwardly appear righteous unto men, but within ye are full of hypocrisy and iniquity."

†   †   †

WHAT is a religious life? I would answer, the life lived day by day by a Christian man. This im-mediately raises another question, namely, what is a Christian man? Not one who lives in a Christain land. If I lived in China it would not necessarily follow that I was a Confucian. Not one who lives a

18

moral life. The Brahmin & Buddhist do that. Being a church member does not make a man a Christian. For an answer to this question we must turn to the text book on Christianity—the Bible. Here we discover a Christian is a disciple of Jesus Christ. That is to say—one who sits at the feet of Jesus to learn of him. The Christian must obey Jesus, worship Jesus, live Jesus. This the early Christian sought to do. Modern necessities have not abrogated these conditions. What is a Christian man? By profession he is one who receives Jesus Christ as revealed in the Bible; who commits his soul to the keeping of Christ; rests his eternal hope upon the atonement of Christ; believes & confesses publicly his belief to this end. As to *character*, he aims to exemplify the principles of the golden rule and the sermon on the mount. His aspirations are to place his feet in the footprints of his master. As to *occuption*, he undertakes the beneficent work of Christ. He goes where suffering is; visits the afflicted; relieves the distressed; comforts the sorrowing; inspires the despairing; saves the lost.

† † †

IS there anything incompatible with this view of a religious life and real manhood? Assuredly not. History of the past and present furnishes abundant proof of my position. Many of the grandest men of history were Christian men. In whatever realm we look, whether among soldiers, statesmen, scientists, musicians, painters, sculptors, poets or authors, we find those whose names are household words, who were devoted Christians—men who lived the religious life in the highest sense of the word. What higher type of real manhood has this country developed than that exemplified in the life and death of our martyr president Wm. McKinley? As a soldier, a citizen, as statesman, & as the chief executive of this great nation, he was always and first a man! Wm. McKinley all his life was a religious man and his death affords one of the sublimest testimonies to the power of the Christian experience and faith that the world has in recent years witnessed.

Wm. E. Gladstone, acknowledged by friends & foes to be the greatest statesman the last century produced was a religious man. The world has had fewer men who were more devout and earnest as followers of Jesus than Wm. E. Gladstone.

Sometimes young men are tempted to sneer at the religious life as something for women and children—but not a thing for men of brain and muscle. Would it not be a greater indication of brain and strength to be reverential towards that God before whom Isaac Newton and Kepler, & Prof. Silliman, and Joseph Henry, and Louis Agassiz were not ashamed to bow? Herschel staggered back from his telescope exhausted and overwhelmed, unable any longer to look at the display of God's omnipotence!

† † †

WHERE must we look today for the leaders in athletics? Without question in the ranks of the Young Men's Christian Association. No less than 300 men, educated, refined and possessing the highest types of physical manhood, and devoting their entire time to the development of athletic and physical culture, are connected with this organization in this country, who live devoted religious lives. Stagg, the famous English athlete gave up fame and fortune to devote his life to lead other young men into a religious life. Geo. E. Crowdis the famous left-guard of Princeton's varsity Team of 96-97-98 was a pronounced Christian man, and is today a preacher of the gospel in Indiana, & one of the finest types of physical manhood I have ever seen.

Wm. A. Sandy, once a famous base ball player, is now an evangelist of marvellous power & ability. When we turn to another characteristic of character that appeals to young men — physical bravery, we find here abundant testimony in favor of a religious life.

Major Geo. O. O. Howard (retired) is a veteran of the civil war, and an ex-Indian fighter of courage and success. All through the civil war & his more than twenty-five years of service since, he was known, far & wide as a most earnest Christain man. Few men have a better record for bravery, on the field of battle, than General Howard. Not only did he possess physical courage, but he had moral courage, which is the highest type of courage. When a student at West Point at the very beginning of his cadetship he took his stand before his mates altho' subjected to their scorn and ridicule thereby. I heard him tell of his first battle with himself at that time. He had just entered the Academy

20

and when summoned to the chapel service the question arose in his mind as to whether he would carry his Bible across the campus before the other fellows or not. He decided to show his colors at once. That was real courage. Speaking of West Point brings to mind a recent happening there. Last June, President Roosevelt visited the Academy, and among other things he did there, was the decoration of Cadet Calvin Pearl Titus with a medal of honor for bravery. Cadet Titus was a bugler of the 14th Infantry, U.S.A. during the troubles in China. On August 14th 1900, he was the first to scale the walls at Peking. His brave act was witnessed by thousands and commented on by the press of the country. Cadet Titus was, and is a religious young man. The night of his enlistment for the Spanish-American War, he was assigned to a tent with half a dozen men, and when it came time for retiring, he said, looking about, "I don't know as any of you men pray, but I do," and he went down on his knees. Titus is a Christian man, but he is also a brave and manly man. Never in the history of the West Point Military Academy has a "plebe" or any cadet been so honored as to be presented with a medal by vote of Congress. His religious life and character did not prevent him from being popular with his fellow cadets, on the contrary he is among the most popular, and takes a leading part in the religious work of the Academy.

I HAVE said that young men often have a mistaken idea concerning a religious life. They fail to grasp the truth that it is the natural life. Herbert Spencer, in his *Data of Ethics*, declares anything a success or a failure in view of the degree to which it performs the distinctive function for which it was intended.

No intelligent man can dispute the fact that man is "the crown of creation;" that he is a living soul made in the image of God. Is it not true then that the true measure of a man's life is the extent to which he "conforms to the image of His Son?"

It was my privilege last June to hear a masterly address on "What is a Christian Man?" by Dr. Howard Agnew Johnston of New York, who in speaking to this point said; "A man may be a tailor's model; some men measure manhood by millinery. A man may be an athletic giant; some men measure manhood by muscle. A man may be a social lion; some men measure manhood by manners. A man may be big in Wall Street; some men measure manhood by money. Intellect, thought, genius, may be the goal of another's ambitions; some men measure manhood by mind; morals may even be regarded as the measure of a man; but unless he shall rise above all this, he has not risen to God's measure of a man, and he is a failure as an immortal soul. The distinctive thing for which he was created he has failed to develop to the full capacity with which God has endowed him."

These thoughts suggest the words of Him the wisest of all men who said; "For what is a man profited, if he shall gain the whole world and lose his own soul?"

The young man who turns away from a religious life expresses his unbelief in the teachings of the Bible and adopts a course that is ruinous. Why? Because he will soon lose faith in the highest and best things of life. This loss of faith whether in domestic life, in the commercial world, or in religion produces disaster and robs life here, and hereafter, of its choicest rewards.

THE MAN AND HIS BOOKS
REVIEWS & REMARKS ON BOOKS
AND READING; CONDUCTED BY

FREDERICK BENJAMIN

Success in Print

WE are overburdened, for the moment, with books, papers and magazines of the "helpful" sort; all done into type to the glory & profit of their authors and publishers, and for the uplifting of young men. "Success" is the cry of the hour. Advice, suggestion, inspiration, precept and example are thrust at us in type and cartoon, by lecture and conversation.

This would be a great thing for us young men if it were not for one objection — it very soon becomes a case of "too many cooks" and too much cooking.

The young man who reads the many formulas for growing successful, finds them so various that he is completely at sea. Instead of one straight and narrow path, he finds every sign-board upon every road and by-way pointing "To Success," and nearly all of them are so cunningly contrived that he is led to believe the City Beautiful to be just beyond the first turning... Or he falls into a worse error & becomes so stimulated by reading accounts of the other fellow's reward and method of climbing, that he is fair drunk with dreams and sinks back among his pillows to babble the magic word "Success! Success!" as though the simple sound would lift him from his small clerkship into a position of trust and wealth and honor.

Bah!

Quit reading "How to Succeed" and do something. Read books that amuse, that teach you new facts concerning your business; read poetry if you can stand it, and some good histories such as Fiske wrote. But restrict this reading of *Excelsior*, & try to sell more goods, keep neater books or drive a shrewder bargain.

The Young Man in Modern Life

by Beverley Warner

AMONG my friends it is always my pleasure to number one or two clergymen—men who felt themselves called to sacrifice their pleasure to their faith; their worldly and practical success to an ill-paid ideal of helpfulness. These men, when the professional priestly air is cast off to give place to that *comeradarie* of a pipe by firelight, have proven themselves the most solid of companions. Their trade leads them to know the troubles of the world: they watch the flight of souls into the unknown; they listen to sorrows and confessions; they see want & misery, and riches and misery; and their tempers are softened by the trial.

Such a clergyman wrote *The Young Man in Modern Life*. He has been through the fire, not only upon his own account, but with others. He offers his experience and best thought to young men who are facing their problems; yet realizing his helplessness to do more than advise, he says, "You must live your own life. Others may sacrifice for you, and even die for you, but they can't live for you."

And herein is the chiefest difference between Dr. Warner and so many others who write for the benefit of the new generation — he realizes that he can only be a friend to suggest; whereas the others lay down a schedule of rules and smother us in unasked advice.

Dr. Warner's book is divided into

chapters dealing very plainly with the most vital points in young manhood — Surroundings, Work, Amusements, Books, Marriage and Religion. His thoughts, especially those upon Work, are sane and practical. They are liberally tinged with Christianity but not with creed; they are the thoughts of a man to whom God is a reality to be acknowledged seven days in the week instead of one, yet never a word of the goody-goody sort is uttered.

One closes the book as one would bid good-night to an old and honored friend—glad of the meeting and stronger for the kindly sympathy of a strong mind.

(The Young Man in Modern Life. by Beverley Warner. 85 cents net: postage 9 cents.   Dodd, Mead and Co., New York. 1902.)

Any book noted in this department will be sent postpaid by THE YOUNG MEN'S HOME JOURNAL, except *net* books, upon which postage is extra.

DON'T DRINK

DR. George Herschell, of London, has recently written a book, entitled, *Health Troubles of City Life*, that is highly praised by London critics. In a chapter devoted to the study of stimulants he says :—

Stimulants never increase the natural capacity of the brain. They can only abstract for the purpose of work in hand some of the energies which, are sorely needed to repair & restore a brain which has already been taxed to the furthest limit which is consistent with health. To remove the sense of fatigue caused by overwork by the consumption of alcohol is to close one's ears to the voice of nature. The weariness of the brain is a protest against further exertion until recuperation has been obtained by rest; and if the weary feeling is deadened or destroyed by adventitious means nature will exact her penalty.

When the overworked man of business having been on his legs all day, and feeling fit to drop, with a sensation of "all-goneness" about the region of the stomach, rouses himself with whatever he is in the habit of taking, be it *whisky, champagne,* or even *tea or coffee,* he *does not add* one atom of force *to his stock of energy,* although he fancies he does, but having put to sleep his sense of weariness, *simply appropriates some of his reserve for the present necessity.* He has accepted a bill at short date to which a ruinous rate of interest is attached, and his resources will not allow him to make many repetitions of the experiment. His account at the bank of life will soon be withdrawn. Alcohol cannot add one iota to his reserve of nervous energy, but it may *delude him into exhausting it.* The busy man should once for all rid himself of this fancy that he can create by artificial means an abnormal store of brain power. He cannot enlarge the limits which nature has set up,

EDITORIAL.

A MAN of deep thinking is usually one who doesn't talk much. Still waters run deep. A silent man has many advantages over a talkative one. He will frequently conceal his ignorance behind his silence and receive credit for knowing more than he knows. A talkative man is usualy of shallow mind. He talks merely for talking's sake. His words are received at his own low appraisal and his opinions & advice are not regarded seriously. He is likely to say many things that might better have been left unsaid and indulge in angry and disagreeble remarks which in his quieter moments he may have reason to regret. To this talkative class belongs the man with the Argument. Suggest a subject and he instantly takes the affirmative or the negative & challenges you to debate! He will argue to show why he is right and when you admit it, he will argue that you are wrong in admitting it! To this class belongs also the Fault Finder and Carping Critic. He must talk about something, and not being well informed on important and substantial matters, he must needs indulge in small talk.

This aimless, meaningless, time-wasting habit of talking is a pernicious one and should be carefully guarded against. Thoughts held within the mind are dangerous enough, but once expressed no power can possibly recall them. Carleton well expresses it:

Boys flying kites haul in their white-winged birds:
You can't do that way when you're flying words.
"Careful with fire," is good advice we know;
"Careful with words," is ten times doubly so.
Thoughts unexpress'd may sometimes fall back dead,
But God Himself can't kill them once they're said!

There is no chance, no destiny, no fate,
Can circumvent or hinder or control
The firm resolve of a determind soul.
Ella Wheeler Wilcox.

IN building a house, a character or a business, much depends upon the foundation. To erect a costly building upon sand is an unwise thing & yet this is what thousands of people are doing daily. I was on an island recently during a severe storm of wind and rain and after it was over I noticed that a large house that apparently stood strong and secure a few moments before, had been turned partly over, the windows all broken and the posts that had supported it knocked from under. It had been built upon sand. When I entered the building I observed shattered walls, broken beams, bulging floors and every indication of the work of a cyclone.

I walked up the shaky stairway & found the same condition of things there. Dizzy from looking at this house turned upsidedown, I wondered if the owner had ever read these words: "And he shall be likened unto a foolish man, which builded his house upon the sand; and the rain descended, and the floods came, and the winds blew, and beat upon that house; and it fell: and great was the fall of it." A practical builder told me afterwards the building would be a total loss & that it was the result of a poor foundation. The lesson is is that when you build a house, and particularly the physical temple in which you expect to dwell for four-score years or more, see to it that you are like the wise man "which builded his house upon a rock; and the rain descended, and the floods came, & the winds blew, and beat upon that house; and it fell not: for it was founded upon a rock." If you wish to build a character to stand the test of time, see to it that you get down into the depths until you have struck rock. Some things that enter into a good foundation are integrity, honor, courage, sympathy, manliness, truth and love. If you are going into business, find out the fundamental principles governing it and master them. Put your personal character into its foundation and proceed to erect your building slowly and cautiously and always with regard to its security and permanency.

THE keynote of true greatness is simplicity. In all ages this quality has been a prominent char-acteristic of great minds. Simplicity in tatse & desire means increased opportunity for doing something for others. The tendency of the present day is towards simplicity in art, literature, dress, language, etc. Along these lines of simplicity we can get many valuable lessons from the lives of distinguished men. An exceptional example in this respect is to be found in the character of William Cullen Bryant, the secret of whose success and longevity may be easily discerned from the following letter written by him in 1871 to his friend, Joseph H. Richards, Esq.:

To Joseph H. Richards, Esq.,

Dear Sir: I promised, sometime since, to give you some account of my habits of life, so far, at least, as regards diet, exercise, and occupation. I am not sure that it will be of any use to you, although the system which I have for many years observed seems to answer my purpose very well. I have reached a pretty advanced period of life, without the usual infirmities of old age, & with my strength, activity, & bodily faculties generally in pretty good preservation. How far this may be the effect of my way of life, adopted long ago, & steadily adhered to, is perhaps uncertain.

I rise early, at this time of the year about five thirty; in the summer, half an hour, or even an hour, earlier. Immediately, with very little incumbrance of clothing, I begin a series of exercises, for the most part designed to expand the chest, and at the same time call into action all the muscles and articulations of the body. These are performed with dumb-bells, the very lightest, covered with flannel; with a pole, a horizontal bar and a light chair swung around my head. After a full hour, and sometimes more, passed in this maner, I bathe from head to foot. When at my place in the country, I sometimes shorten my exercises in the chamber, and going out, occupy myself for half an hour or more in some work which requires brisk exercise. After my bath, if breakfast be not ready, I sit down to my studies until I am called.

My breakfast is a simple one—hominy and milk, or, in place of hominy, brown bread, or oatmeal, or wheaten grits, and, in the season, baked sweet apples. Buckwheat cakes I do not decline, nor any other article of vegetable food, but animal food I never take at breakfast. Tea and coffee I never touch at any time. Sometimes I take a cup of chocolate, which has no narcotic effect, and agrees with me very well. At breakfast I often take fruit, either in its natural state or freshly stewed.

After breakfast I occupy myself for a while with my studies, and then, when in town, I walk down to the office of the Evening Post, nearly three miles distant, and after about three hours, return, always walking, whatever be the weather or the state of the streets. In the country I am engaged in my literary tasks till a feeling of weariness drives me out into the open air, and I go upon my farm or into the garden & prune the trees, or perform some other work about them which they need, and then go back to my books. I do not often drive out, preferring to walk.

In the country I dine early, and it is only at that meal that I take either meat or fish, & of these but a moderate quantity, making my dinner mostly of vegetables. At the meal which is called "tea," I take only a little bread and butter, with fruit, if it be on the table. In town, where I dine later, I take but two meals a day. Fruit makes a considerable part of my diet, and I eat it at almost any part of the day without inconvenience. My drink is water, yet I sometimes, though rarely, take a glass of wine. I am a natural Temperance man, finding myself rather confused than exhilarated by wine. I never meddle with tobacco, except to quarrel with its use.

That I may rise early, I, of course, go to bed early: in town, as early as ten; in the country, somewhat earlier. For many years I have avoided in the evening every kind of literary occupation which tasks the faculties, such as composition, even to the writing of letters, for the reason that it excites the nervous system and prevents sound sleep.

My brother told me, not long since, that he had seen in a Chicago newspaper, and several other Western journals, a paragraph in which it is said that I am in the habit of taking quinine as a stimulant; that I have depended upon the excitement it produces in writing my verses, and that in consequence of using it in that way I had become as deaf as a post. As to my deafness, you know that to be false, and the rest of the story is equally so. I abominate all drugs and narcotics, and have always carefully avoided everything which spurs nature to exertions which it would not otherwise make. Even with my food I do not take the usual condiments, such as pepper, and the like.

I am, sir, truly yours,

W. C. Byrant.

New York, March 30, 1871.

This letter couched in simple language contains the essence of true living and may be summed up as follows:

1. Early rising.
2. Daily physical exercise.
3. Daily bathing.
4. Simple food.
5. Daily study.
6. Long walks.
7. Keeping in touch with nature.
8. Total abstinence from liquor, tobacco and drugs.

Study this letter carefully for yourself. It helped me and it can help you.

A Letter From The Interior

By *AN OUTSIDER*

MY name is Indiana Schreck-engost—an' say, haint thet a corker! Me an' mi name is twins. Haint nobody never hearn o' nither one. And by crackey, there's the darndest part o' the hull thing. Wot i want's the youniversal asteme o' the popouliss. And gosh dern the luck, I haint got ut. Not yit, that is. Wot is more, 'taint likely that i'll git ut, nither, no, not if i live a hundred years more still. And i aint like tu du thet on a 20 aker farm — no, not a tenth of ut, not a fefth, not even a 3d of ut.

"Wot is life!" thet's what I says to Mandy, I says, yistiddy a week ago come Tuesdy. Thet's what I sez. I says, "I feel like goin' to war and shootin' my convictiations through a gun. Here I set," I says, "kind of an unwiseacre, you might say. An' right next door a young feller thet knows so plaguey little thet he'd dround in the A, B, Seas if the school marm didn't hist him out and sorter paddle his canoe fer him. And 'for you can sow oats twict in the same field, blessed if that cuss hasn't gone & git hisself 'lected tresurer of Pensylvany or somethin—head of some Life Insurance, mebby. Or any ways," I says, "he's got money now, and with money—providin' you've got enough of ut, you never can do no wrong. The Lord," I says, "is on the side o' the biggest bank account," I says. "Because it says 'The Lord loveth a chereful giver,' an them's the only kind that can give chereful nowadays. How they git ut all beats me — some on 'em wouldn't even make a first rate pall bearer, they're so plaguey dumb. They'll come an' visit you, though, fer six weeks hand runnin', all the while instructin' you and givin' you to understand what a slow sort o' life your livin'." Thet s what I sez to Mandy.

Ez if I didn't know thet areddy. Ain't I posted on what a dern day time of it I've got in this worl'? It's a bum place, this worl' is — 'taint no show in ut fer a honest man no more. Jist to show you what sort of a chanct they give a feller to git up in his biznes — Onct I writ to Cy Henry to git me an apointmint in somethink or other, so's I could git a start, sorter, & forge up like the rest on 'em. Cy, he writ back thet he'd tumble all over himself to do more'n I assed him to. And every day then I drove tew mile to the pust offis for a letter from Cy tellin' me to come. Thet was 'leven year back, and he aint writ yet. Onct he come back to these parts an' I drove over to where he was astayin an' I sez to him, "Cy," says I, "thet dozen of appintmints what ye sent me tuckered out," I says. "When ye go back to New York why jist send me up another gross, will ye?" I says sarcastic like. An' he swore up & down thet he'd git me one sure pop. But he aint never done it. So I've maid up my mind now that ef you're a smart sort o' cuss why the worl' will give you a great deal tu be shure,—it will give you all the time you want and all the advice you don't want. And that's about all you'll git fer nawthin'. Otherwise, ef you want anything you've got to git ut fer yourself.

An' I jes' want ter tell you, too, thet thair haint a feller ever so low down, I don't care hoo he is, but thet their feller wants to git up in the worl' and be suthin' or to'ther. It's jest born in 'em. I knowed that long ago from my own ixperience, and I seen it in print sinct. Some gurl out west, name o' Mary Mac Lane, has writ all about ut in a book, & wot is in print is so. Don't know when i have looked in a boock thet kindo' said just what I'd 'a' said my own self if th' Almighty'd 'a' gave me the gift o' penwork.

Ja know? When I was 19 I was jist thet way myself— like this here Mary says she is now — i thot I was jist ekil to anythink thet would turn up. And Lord how I did ache fer suthin' tu turn up! Me and Bill Peters used ter talk ut all over how we wuz goin' to be these here millionairs that ye read so much about. Bill thot he was a heap smarter nor I wuz— an' Lord, I never said nothin' but ut made me snicker up my sleeve to hear thet feller talk knowin' how easy I was gonto walk right on ahead of him and one day take him ridin' on my

steam yawt. That was 20 year back. Bill's tendin' store now fer Mosie Patterson over tu Buckville, an' i have my 20 akers. But say, that there Mary McLane has spoke out jist what a man feels while he's jist naturally waitin' 20 year fer suthin' to turn up. We all feels thet way, I reckon. It's all powerful true, whut Mary says. An' I bet you Mary thinks all the while how smart she is coz she's writ that boock — when tain't nothin' but jist wot everybody that's pushed down in this cruel worl' could rite if they only knowed how tu spell.

Mary, she rites elegant like and sad,—"Never does the pitiable barren emptiness of my life come upon me with so intense a force as when my eyes light up at the site of them six tooth brushes in the bathroom. Every Friday an' every Friday to see nawthink but them there six pesky tooth brushes — why its sutthin offle!" That's jist it. Ja know? I started out same as that Mary, a thinkin' 'at i wuz suthin' worth while, 't i was "it," an' ace high, an' all thet. And now i go out over mi 20 akers and look at them weeds, or the weat is down mebby,-knocked down by a storm, er else the dry weather is puckerin' ut all up — jist them 'ere 20 akers an' no more. An' then i look down at mi torn breeches! And then i go in an' set down and rede about how this here J. Beerpoint Morgin's jist spent $600,000 fer a picter, & how the hull popyouliss salooted this or that emprer, and I say to Mandy how ut dew beat all. I say ut's a derned outrage that wile them fellers is ridin' roun' in their barooshes that here me and Mandy's got to set an' see nawthink but the corn dyin' on these dried up 20 akers — nawthink but jist them 20—an' ut's poor ground too boot. "It's a dern shame, that's wot ut is," I say over and over agin. Wy wasn't i born King of England? or wy aint i made mi millyons? er wy is ut, hanyow, thet I've got ter set here all day long seein' nawthink but these here 20 akers? That's wot I want to know. 'Taint right— not by a long shot. This worl's all wrong. They aint no show no more fer an honest man.

But this here Mary MacLane's gave me an idear. If she can raise a row about it, wy i can tew, by golly. And so, I thot'i'd rite tew you and ast you ef you new wear I could find a feller to print a little suthin' an' how mutch I'd likely git out of ut. Coz I haint agointo take no trouble fer nawthink. But ef there's any chanct o' gettin' anythink printed, an' any chanct o' makin' suthin' out of ut, wy i'm there every time, you bet. Wouln't ut be a joke ef one o' these days I'd be ridin' Bill Peters around in my yawt yet, made my fortion outa ritin' wot a cruil and barren & offle place this yere worl's grown to be? Eh, Bill?

THOUGHTS FOR THE THOUGHTLESS

Never walk one way and look another.

That which is "too much trouble" now, may be much more trouble after while.

Never jump off a moving train.

Success comes from not making the same mistake twice.

Next to a kindly act, is the appreciation thereof.

If there is anything in a man his opportunity will come sooner or later.

The best antedote for sorrow is steady occupation.

The strong man is weak if he lacks confidence in himself.

Those who reprove us are often more valuable as friends than those who flatter us.

PRINCETON
PREPARATORY SCHOOL

The advantages of specialization in education are as great as in any other sphere of human activity. This school is for boys, older than fourteen, that are preparing for college. Some of the features of the plan: No time wasted in unrequired studies; individual instruction as from a tutor; no boy is kept back or unduly hurried because of his classmates' needs. For illustrated circular address

J. B. FINE, HEADMASTER
PRINCETON, NEW JERSEY

THE WASHINGTON SCHOOL FOR BOYS.
Washington, D. C.

Each boy is expected to be a gentleman. To this end his surroundings are made those of a gentleman, and the modes of the life of which he is a part will be such as befit a gentleman. "Manners maketh Man," and environment manners. For full particulars, address the Head Master

TRINITY SCHOOL.
139-147 West 91st St., New York.

Catalogue upon request.   Rev. August Ulman, D.D., Rector.

NEW YORK PREPARATORY SCHOOL.
15 West 43rd St., New York.

Regents and College Examinations. Day Evening or Private. Send for catalogue. Telephone 4696 — 38.

MT. PLEASANT MILITARY ACADEMY.
Ossining-on-Hudson, N. Y.

Founded 1814. References: Hon. Jos. H. Choate, Hamilton W. Mabie, L. H. D., Chas. B. Hubbell, formerly Prest. Board of Education, New York City. For beautifully illustrated year book address THE PRINCIPALS.

BERKELEY SCHOOL.
New location, 6 west 75th St. N. Y.

Triennial catalog will be sent on application. Personal calls received between 9 & 12; at other times by appointment. JOHN STUART WHITE, LL.D. Head Master. J. CLARK READ, A. M. Registrar.

31 FIFTH AVENUE NEW YORK

OPEN ALL THE YEAR
PUBLIC MATINEES
EVERY INSTRUCTOR A SPECIALIST

FULL and PARTIAL COURSES

WRITE for ILLUSTRATED CATALOGUE

Adeline Stanhope Wheatcroft   :   :   :   Director

www.ingramcontent.com/pod-product-compliance
Lightning Source LLC
Chambersburg PA
CBHW061059050726
47592CB00004B/1753